GREENFIELD PUBLIC LIBRARY

DATE DUE

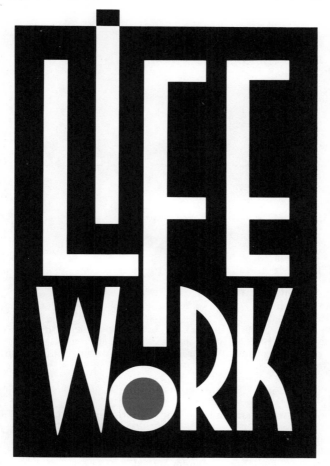

A WORKBOOK
For Adult Children of Alcoholics

Sally Coleman, M.A., N.C.A.C.
Rita J. Donley, Ph.D.

CompCare Publishers

2415 Annapolis Lane
Minneapolis, Minnesota 55441

Library of Congress Cataloging-in-Publication Data
Coleman, Sally
       Lifework, a workbook guide for adult children of alcoholics/ by Sally
Coleman and Rita Donley.
       p. cm.
ISBN 0-89638-264-8
1. Adult children of alcoholics. I. Donley, Rita. II. Title.   362.29Y COL 01
[DNLM: 1. Alcoholism—psychology.   2. Child of Impaired Parents.   3. Parent-
Child Relations.   WM 274 C692L]
HV5132.C63   1992
362.29'23—dc20   91-48275
                                                                      CIP

Cover design by Jeremy Gale

Inquiries, orders, and catalog requests should be addressed to:
CompCare Publishers
2415 Annapolis Lane
Minneapolis, Minnesota 55441
Call 800/328-3330 toll free or
612/559-4800

6	5	4	3	2	1
97	96	95	94	93	92

▦ CONTENTS ▦

THREE

FOUR

FIVE

APPENDIX

⌘ ACKNOWLEDGMENTS ⌘

We acknowledge our clients at the University of Notre Dame Counseling Center and in our private practices for inspiring *Lifework*. Our direction in writing *Lifework* flowed from the progress and courageous changes we continually see occurring in the lives of our hard-working clients. We are grateful for their gift of allowing us to be present as they journey through their path of recovery.

We thank the staff of the University of Notre Dame Counseling Center for providing a climate that we've been able to be creative and develop professionally in.

We also acknowledge and thank our editors, Rosanne Bane, Jane Noland, and Margaret Marsh for their direction and excellent suggestions.

Finally, we wish to give a very heartfelt thank you to the "Chicago Angel" who initially made *Lifework* a reality.

▦ ONE ▦

Getting the Help
You Need

Lifework has been written to help adult children of alcoholics and others who grew up with family dysfunctions begin a journey of healing and affirmation. This workbook is designed for you to personalize as you use it in the weeks ahead. You will find places to record the landmarks of your recovery and healing. It is our special wish that you see completing your *Lifework*, not as another form of 'homework,' but as a valuable, growth-producing experience.

Lifework was originally designed as a support tool for people in adult children of alcoholics therapy groups, but it can also be successfully used by individuals in ACoA or ACA Twelve Step groups, and by those who are working individually with a therapist. Many adult children feel a great deal of pain about feeling different and, because participation in a group can alleviate this pain, we generally feel that optimum healing occurs in the group experience.

You might be thinking that you couldn't possibly talk about your pain and concerns to one person, let alone a whole group. Most adult children feel this way. It is difficult for everyone to know what to say or how much to trust when meeting a group of people in a therapy situation for the first time. As the group members grow in their willingness to share their experiences and learn healthy ways to respond to each other, trust builds and the group environment becomes more and more comfortable and healing. However, there are circumstances, listed below, in which a person can benefit more from individual therapy.

When to Seek Individual Therapy

1. ***If you have never been in therapy before.*** You may want to start with individual therapy if you have no previous experience with therapy. It may be important for you to form a safe relationship with a therapist and have the opportunity to talk about your history and your reasons for seeking therapy before beginning group. Feeling "listened to" in individual therapy can lay the foundation for future group experiences and help you identify appropriate goals for your group work.

2. ***If you have sensitive issues you don't feel comfortable sharing with a group.*** When people begin working through extremely sensitive issues, such as sexual, emotional, or physical abuse, they may feel especially exposed and vulnerable and in need of a one-to-one relationship with a therapist to support them. If some of your past experiences feel too overwhelming to share with a group, at least initially, you may want to begin with individual therapy.

3. ***If you have multiple problems that are severely life-disrupting.*** It may be in your best interest to work on multiple issues with an individual therapist before entering a group, particularly if you feel your life is very unsettled because of these problems. Keep in mind that people with active alcoholism, other drug dependence, or other addictions require proper treatment before their adult children work can truly begin. Those who are also addicted will need to pay special attention to maintaining recovery from the addiction throughout their adult children work.

4. ***If you are extremely afraid of participating in a group.*** While it is natural for everyone to have some hesitancy at the beginning of a group experience, if the fear becomes

so extreme that you are unwilling or unable to share and participate in a group, individual counseling is recommended. Through your adult children of alcoholics work, you can learn to understand and manage this fear.

5.   *If you have experienced extreme social deprivation and isolation.* Some adult children grow up so socially and emotionally isolated that they don't really know how to interact with others. They seem to lack basic communication and other social skills that are needed to function with some ease in most situations. If this is your experience, working with a therapist on an individual basis can help you identify which skills you lack and how that has affected your life. With your therapist's help, you can then set goals and begin to learn to feel more secure when interacting with others. Once you develop some confidence, participating in a therapy group will give you excellent opportunities to enhance your social skills in a safe environment.

If you believe some of these circumstances apply to you, talk it over with a therapist. Like most people, you will find that, after working with a therapist one-to-one, sometimes for a short time, sometimes for a longer period, you'll eventually be prepared to take advantage of the additional healing that comes from participating in a therapy group.

Selecting a Therapist

Whether you will be meeting with a therapist for individual or group sessions, there are guidelines for choosing a person you can trust and work effectively with. In general, a good therapist is one that makes you feel:

1.   *Safe:* Your work as an adult child who grew up with alcoholism or other dysfunctions in your family will include expressing a range of strong emotions as you grieve through your experiences. It is essential that your therapist encourage you to feel the sadness, anger, and joy. You need to feel safe enough in the therapy setting to "take the lid off" your emotions as you express your feelings and share your deepest secrets.

2. **Listened to:** It is important that you feel your therapist listens to what you're saying. You may not always agree with or like some of your therapist's interpretations and suggestions, but if you feel safe and heard you will be able to trust him or her enough to look deeper into your own reactions and resistances.

3. **Validated:** Everyone has good qualities and special gifts, and one of the primary goals of therapy is to help you recognize and accept your worth. It will be much easier for you to look at your difficulties and problems if you know your therapist recognizes and affirms that you are a valuable, unique person.

4. **Protected by clear boundaries:** In your initial family, boundaries may have been confused and poorly defined. For example, you may have been expected to act like the parent for your parent(s) or your siblings. Or your parent(s) might have been sexually inappropriate with you. Or you felt responsible for everyone else's feelings and for making sure their lives were okay. Therefore, it is very important that your therapist establish clear and appropriate boundaries in your relationship. It is not appropriate or healing for you to have a friendship or intimate relationship with your therapist.

5. **Understood and respected:** You have the right to expect expert support from your therapist. Therapists who have been trained in the field of addiction counseling are better equipped to understand and support you in your work as an adult child. Those who also have extensive training in the dynamics and process of individual and group therapy are usually the most effective.

Choosing a Group

In your community, there may be adult children of alcoholics therapy groups as well as Twelve Step ACoA or ACA, CODA, and Al-Anon groups. Both therapy and Twelve Step groups offer adult children a valuable place to learn, share, and heal, but there are differences detailed below. Some adult children make time to participate in both therapy and Twelve Step groups.

Distinctions between Therapy and Twelve Step Groups

	Adult Children Therapy Groups	ACoA or ACA Twelve Step Groups
Philosophy	Members explore personal issues in depth through individual and group dynamics.	Members attend meetings based on the principles of Alcoholics Anonymous (AA) and learn how to incorporate the Twelve Steps of recovery into their daily lives.
Structure	Members and leaders support, validate, and interpret by sharing their reactions.	Counseling, advice-giving, or reacting during meetings is discouraged. Members relate only by sharing their own "experience, strength, and hope."
Size	Usually 8–10 members.	Meeting size varies.
Duration	Usually 6–12 months.	Ongoing. Most members view Twelve Step programs as a continuing life experience.
Leaders	One or two therapists with appropriate credentials.	No formal leaders. Chairperson changes each week.
Cost	Fees vary. Group treatment may be covered through health insurance.	Self-supporting through member contributions. No dues or fees required.
Confidentiality	Group members make a commitment to refrain from discussing any group information outside of the group meetings.	Anonymity is a basic principle of all Twelve Step programs and most members choose to be identified by their first names only. The slogan that best illustrates this principle is: "Who you see here, what you hear here, when you leave here, let it stay here."

Considerations in Choosing a Group

If you decide to participate in a therapy group, you should consider the following:

1. **_Therapists:_** Who is facilitating the group? What are their backgrounds, training, and experience in adult children issues? Will they attend all sessions, monitor the group's activities, encourage honest sharing, intervene when appropriate, take action on the behalf of members who feel threatened, and in other ways create a safe atmosphere of mutual respect and trust?

2. **_Fees:_** How much will this cost and how much is covered by your insurance?

3. **_Structure and duration:_** What is the format for meetings? Will the group have a definite beginning and ending or will it continue indefinitely? Will the group allow new members to join at any time? What are the therapists' expectations about attendance and members who decide to leave group? How well do these elements fit your needs and preferences?

While all Twelve Step groups are based on the original Twelve Steps of Alcoholics Anonymous, there is a range of group formats. It is suggested that you try several different meetings until you find one that feels comfortable and safe. We also recommend that you attend at least six meetings before deciding if this is a tool you can use in your recovery.

If you decide to join a Twelve Step ACoA or ACA, CODA, or Al-Anon group, you should consider the following:

1. **_Group structure:_** Do group members rotate responsibility for the meeting? Or is there evidence of an unhealthy pattern of one or two "leaders" who dominate the group?

2. **_Boundaries:_** Do group members respect each other's boundaries by avoiding cross talk, interrupting, gossip, and advice-giving?

3. **_Sponsor support:_** Are there people who've grown in their recovery and are willing to sponsor new members?

4. **_Consistency:_** Can you count on a consistent meeting time, location, format, and shared hope of recovery?

5. **_Safety:_** Do you feel safe, whether you leave a meeting feeling more positive and upbeat or leave recognizing that you need to go through a painful experience to continue your healing?

In both therapy and Twelve Step groups, you should be aware of and respect the principles of confidentiality and healthy participation. Group members have a mutual commitment to protect each other by agreeing not to divulge details that would identify others outside of group. It is okay to share your own experience with friends or family, but it is not okay to discuss other members in any way. While there is no guarantee of confidentiality in either type of group, it has been our experience that members of both groups respect each other's privacy. Keep in mind that therapists are required by law to respect all information from clients as confidential, except when someone appears to be planning harm to self (suicide) or others (homicide) or when it appears that children or elderly individuals are being abused. In these cases therapists are legally bound to break confidentiality to provide people the assistance they need.

People in groups, both therapy and Twelve Step, should participate on a voluntary basis, sharing only what feels safe and appropriate for them at the time. You should always have the freedom to refuse to participate in any specific activity without fear of consequences from other members or therapists. Do remember, however, that the more you choose to participate, the more you benefit from the group experience.

Frequently, therapy groups will state specifically what commitment is expected from members. Twelve Step programs also work best when we commit to regular, ongoing attendance. It is especially important for new members to select a "home group" and attend that same meeting each week. The fellowship and sense of connectedness found in Twelve Step programs is a vital ingredient in healing and recovery that isn't available when we "meeting-hop."

Also, it helps to attend Twelve Step or therapy meetings with an open mind and listen for the "one thing" you especially relate to, instead of focusing on all the ways we are different from each other. You'll meet many different personalities at meetings and can learn something about yourself from each of them. It has been said that the people you have the strongest reactions to in life are usually your best teachers because they cause you to look inward and discover what is still unsettled in you. In the adult children of alcoholics group experience, you can learn to focus on what is helpful and let go of the rest. Commitment is vital to establishing your own program, through which you can come to experience positive life changes.

Applying *Lifework* in Your Adult Children Work

As previously mentioned, *Lifework* can support you as you work through your adult child issues, whether you choose to pursue individual therapy, group therapy, or Twelve Step participation, or some combination of these.

If you are working with a therapist on an individual basis, *Lifework* can provide information about how alcoholism affected you and your family. As outlined in Chapter Two, recovery is hard work and you have to feel safe to begin. Developing a safe relationship with your therapist and learning how to talk about what happened to you is an important first step. The Path to Recovery, described in Chapter Three, will help you and your therapist assess where you are and where you can go. As you work through the exercises in the Personal Lifework section, you'll have opportunities to remember what it was like to be a child growing up in your family and to process your reactions with your therapist. The Reflections Journal can be used to record your reactions and chart your progress.

When adult children who grew up with family dysfunctions recover, they uncover a lot of old pain that needs to be dealt with. Sometimes it might hurt so much you'll wonder if you'll ever move on. Being able to re-read, in your own words, where you were and how you felt a week or a month ago will help you see your progress. You may still be in pain, but the pain is shifting, and this shift implies movement and growth. For most of us, seeing movement helps us trust that there is light at the end of the tunnel, even if we can't see it yet. If there are adult children therapy groups available in your community, you and your therapist can decide when you are ready to move into group work.

If you are working in an adult children therapy group, *Lifework* provides a common starting place for all members of the group. It provides language to understand what has happened to you and others. When you see other members struggling at various levels on the Path of Recovery, described in Chapter Three, you'll begin to understand the differences in your families of origin and how others react differently to similar experiences.

The exercises and journaling in the Personal Lifework section are designed to help you personalize your recovery. Many times it's helpful to record your reactions to what happened in group or to an important event that occurred between sessions. Group members can use their journaling as a stimulus for ongoing work by reading journal entries to the group or referring to them when they feel stuck. Members can support each other by acknowledging when they see movement by other members on the path of recovery, as well as by declaring their own progress.

Lifework also provides a place to work on your "not yet" category. You may have something you would like to share in group, but don't feel quite ready to do so. Re-reading sections of *Lifework* and writing about this issue will give you preparation time to examine why you are hesitant and what you fear about revealing this issue. Our hope is that you will learn how to bring up any concern without believing you have to have it all figured out. However, especially in the beginning stages of your group work, this structure may provide the support you need to take a risk and let the group know about your struggle.

If you are attending a Twelve Step group, you can use *Lifework* to facilitate writing, one of the tools of recovery mentioned at most meetings. The first sections of *Lifework*, especially Chapter Three, The Path of Recovery, can be analyzed by using the Twelve Steps: What am I powerless over? What do I need to turn over? How do my character defects influence where I am in my recovery? This analysis can be shared with your sponsor as you work the steps. Steps Four, Eight, and Ten all encourage you to take inventories; the Reflections Journal of this book provides a place to do that. Members often take a notebook to Twelve Step meetings to jot down one or two thoughts to reflect on during the week. Keeping track of these bits of wisdom provides you with a mini-meeting between meetings when you need support or comfort.

Some people think that attending Twelve Step meetings

is all they need to do to recover and are not interested in either individual or group therapy, while others prefer to attend meetings in conjunction with therapy. Since an important part of recovery is learning to trust yourself, you will be the best judge of which options will be most beneficial to you.

Whatever path you choose, it is important to acknowledge and affirm your gifts and strengths as well as to recognize how the pain you experienced in your past affects your present life. Just in your willingness to use this workbook and focus on your adult child issues in therapy or a Twelve Step group, you demonstrate your health and desire to grow. Keep this in mind as you work through your pain and grief. By committing yourself to complete the unfinished business from your past, you will enhance your ability to use your gifts to your benefit and the benefit of others.

You won't always feel grief; someday soon you will celebrate your recovery. Adult children of alcoholics and other people who grew up in families that were dysfunctional because of chronic illness or addiction are adaptive survivors who carry from their personal shipwrecks a natural and often untapped abundance of health and wholeness.

▥ TWO ▥

Adult Children Recovery Work

As we said in Chapter One, *Lifework* was originally designed as a support tool for adult children in therapy groups but it can also be used successfully by members of ACoA or ACA Twelve Step groups, and by those working individually with a therapist. We feel that therapy groups provide a great opportunity for recovery, and this chapter is focused on how this recovery can be achieved. People in Twelve Step ACoA groups can adapt some of this material to fit their circumstances. It may be more challenging for an individual and the therapist with whom he or she is working one-to-one to adapt this chapter, since it will be the counselor rather than a group who mirrors and supports the individual's concerns and successes. Still, the groundwork of recovery for adult children from alcoholic or otherwise dysfunctional families is universal.

The tasks that adult children are challenged to accomplish in recovery include:

- becoming honest and taking risks
- giving and receiving validation
- expressing and easing shame

- recognizing and working through grief
- defining personal boundaries
- learning missing skills
  - social skills
  - feelings skills
  - conflict resolution skills
- affirmations
- recognizing and choosing options.

We will talk about these aspects of recovery groundwork in this chapter. But before any adult child can attempt this work, which may seem overwhelming without support, he or she must feel **safe,** have a sense that the work is somehow **relevant** to his or her real life, and **commit** to doing the work.

Safety

It is the work of the group facilitators or the individual therapist to lay the foundation for safety. In Twelve Step groups, there are no recognized leaders, so individuals must be careful to see to their own safety and be aware of group policies or individual behavior that could threaten the progress of all members, while being careful not to "caretake" other members.

In both therapy groups and Twelve Step groups, members enhance safety and each other's progress by committing to a policy of group confidentiality. Each group will establish its own guidelines for confidentiality at the first group meeting so that a feeling of safety can develop in the group as it encourages members to share their real selves. Growing up in a family where there was chronic stress and unpredictable change makes it hard to feel grounded and safe. Sometimes people put on different masks to protect themselves. The place you choose to do your recovery work (individual therapy, group therapy, or a Twelve Step group) is a place to take the masks off and come to know that you will be accepted as you are today.

You are in charge of your recovery work. You have the option of sharing when you are ready. You are encouraged to let yourself be known, but the final decision as to what and when you share will always be yours.

Relevance

In many ways the group will become a model of your family of origin and your current relationships. Certain group members might trigger strong reactions and remind you of people in your past, particularly members of your original family. Initially you might feel very much as you did while you were growing up, and many of these feelings may make you uncomfortable. Yet it is the ability of the group to trigger these uncomfortable feelings and memories that gives it such power to heal.

In the past you may have started to have a feeling or a reaction, but the rules in your family told you, in some way, that to express or acknowledge that feeling or reaction was not permissible. If that happened time after time, eventually you found some way to shut down or numb out that knowledge and learned not to trust yourself. Your recovery work involves returning to a time when you had feelings and reactions, recognizing that the rules are now different, and taking the risk to feel safe enough to acknowledge what is going on inside of you. This is not easy at first. Imagine playing a particular sport for years and being told one day, "All the rules are different." There would definitely be confusion and a period of re-learning.

At first it might be recognizing a physical sensation when someone else is talking, or a brief moment of sadness or anger. You may be quick to dismiss it or feel it is not important enough to examine. Keep in mind that this is a time of exploration. Exploring your feelings each time you notice something new will give you opportunities to know yourself better.

The group will provide a natural climate to point you in the direction of your own "unfinished business." When you listen to another member work through his or her buried grief, you'll learn about your own pain. When you feel deeply sad, angry, or afraid for someone else, it is usually your own pain you feel most strongly. Your reactions to other group members are "internal nudges" that are important to listen to. These nudges are your teachers and you are encouraged to share these reactions as soon as they happen in order to help yourself and others learn. Talking about your reactions will show you and other members how we often stay stuck with our old pain in current relationships. You'll find that healing occurs when you let your true self be known.

Commitment

Commitment is an essential part of your recovery work and will enhance your feelings of safety. In group we ask that members commit to the length of the group and that they make group attendance a priority each week. In some families, commitments weren't regularly honored. Your new adult children group family chooses to honor commitments and to make every effort to "stay together" throughout the process of group work. If a group member truly can't attend a group meeting, that person is asked to contact the facilitators in advance so they can announce his or her absence.

It is especially important that you attend when you don't feel like going. This means that the recovery process is working for you and that you are probably feeling some of the strong initial resistance that naturally accompanies healing. The experience of coming to the group and talking with others about your difficulty in attending is an important part of your growth work.

Becoming Honest and Taking Risks

The secrets adult children carry weigh them down in their daily lives. Your adult children group is a place to get honest with yourself and others. Letting others know the real you is an exciting and liberating experience. It has been found that most group members feel:

> *I have done, thought, and felt things too*
> *bad to share with anyone.*

> *If people really knew me, I would not be*
> *accepted or loved.*

These are myths. Most human beings have had these same feelings, and when they share them with others, they find that they are valued and loved more, not less, and that their honesty is respected. Being part of a "healthy family" means letting the other members know who we really are.

Your history does belong to you and it is your choice when and what you'll share. You will be encouraged to talk as you begin to feel safe and develop trust. The more honest you are and the more you risk, the more you'll be able to grow. It is also important to learn to listen to your intuition and respect your internal pace; you'll know when it's time to share. Sometimes resistance can cloud intuition and keep you silent. It is your willingness to be honest and open with the group that is most important. Some members start talking by sharing how hard it is for them to talk in group. Remember that you can't "pass or fail" group. You are challenged to bring the real you to group.

An example of getting honest and taking a risk might be to acknowledge:

> *I was afraid that sharing my violent fantasies would make them happen.*

Growing up you may not have learned safe and appropriate ways of handling and expressing anger. As a result, you may be uncomfortable with or even unaware of angry feelings. Buried anger may come out in indirect and passive ways, such as overreacting, having periods of violent fantasies, or withdrawing into depression. An adult children group provides a safe environment to practice releasing your anger in safe and direct ways.

Another example of expressing a risk honestly might be admitting:

> *I was so confused about sexuality that I stopped dating.*

Talking about sexuality and sexual concerns is another example of taking a big risk in your therapy group. Accepting the nature of our sexuality is an enormous part of personal growth and development. Sexual fears and secrets can rob us of peace of mind and cause feelings of great shame and confusion. Talking about these fears, guilts, and confusion in a safe environment is a healing experience that will show you that others share the same concerns. Sexual feelings are very powerful and you might be afraid that you'll lose control. As you discuss your concerns with others, you'll come to understand the difference between feelings and actions. Because you have thought and felt something doesn't mean that you are a bad person or that you will lose control and act inappropriately. Learning to talk about sexuality issues helps you put them in perspective.

These two examples may or may not be your biggest concerns. Whatever secrets you are carrying, you will in all likelihood find you are not alone. Taking the risk of being honest will not only further your recovery, it will help you form caring bonds with other members of your group.

Giving and Receiving Validation

Validation lays the groundwork for your recovery. All human beings have a primary and healthy need to hear positive things about themselves. If you have become extremely critical of yourself, you might have a hard time sharing your strengths and gifts with others. It is important to remember that you are a lovable, capable human being with unique talents and gifts. Your strengths and wellness should be continually affirmed in group by the facilitators, group members, and yourself. You will gradually become more comfortable with these positive affirmations and validations. Recognizing your personal worth is an essential goal of your recovery experience and a necessary foundation for healing shame.

In individual therapy, your therapist will encourage you to focus on strengths you have, risks you are taking, and giving yourself credit for the courage it takes to continue focusing on recovery when it is hard and it hurts. Since healthy Twelve Step groups discourage cross talk (commenting on others' feelings or reactions, giving unsolicited advice, or interrupting), it is important to develop a relationship with a sponsor to give you this important channel of feedback and validation. (A sponsor is a person who has been in Twelve Step recovery for a longer period of time and indicates his or her willingness to share experience, strength, and hope with you on an individual basis.) It is important to pick a sponsor you feel safe with, who validates your progress and encourages you to take risks as you work on each of the Twelve Steps.

An example of expressing validation is:

*I'm now able to accept the good things
others say about me.*

Choosing to tell the group, your therapist, or sponsor good things about yourself is the best way to learn about the healing powers of validation. Learning to trust and accept the positive things others tell you is also important. At first, you might be uncomfortable and have a hard time hearing about your goodness, courage, and gifts, but gradually you will begin to love yourself enough to risk accepting praise and compliments. Some people have come from negative environments and have become "comfortable" putting themselves down and minimizing their accomplishments. Part of your ongoing recovery work is working to validate yourself honestly and accept validation from others.

Another example of validation is:

> *Telling other group members about my feelings of caring and respect for them makes me feel like the group is my safe family.*

Validating others is a honest and open way to be attentive to them as they work in the group. As a group member, you will learn to listen with an open mind as others share their stories. You will learn to challenge their nonproductive behaviors and to give honest feedback about their gifts and resources. After another member has shared, you might say, "It took a lot of courage for you to talk about yourself and I feel closer to you now."

Expressing and Easing Shame

Healthy shame is an emotion that all human beings feel to some extent. It is a signal from our conscience, reminding us of the need to set limits and take responsibility for our actions. Chronic shame is the opposite of healthy shame. It is made up of internalized pervasive feelings that come from being severely belittled, judged, blamed, or ignored by others. Healthy shame says, "I made a mistake." Chronic shame says, "I am a mistake." Chronic shame is a feeling of personal worthlessness. When healthy shame allows us to take responsibility for our actions and learn from our mistakes, it can be productive. Chronic shame, on the other hand, often keeps us paralyzed and full of self-loathing.

Shame will be treated gently in group. When it is acknowledged, the healing process flows more easily. You will often find your shame in the "trivial"—in those small moments when you feel "less than." A big part of your work in and out of group will be to discover and share your chronic shame messages. Healing the myth that you are a mistake will open up your "emotional doors" and truly allow you to grieve for your past and be a more effective choice-maker in your daily life. There is space in your Reflections Journal to record shame feelings, messages, and experiences as they are uncovered during your recovery experience and in your daily life.

An example of expressing shame is realizing:

> *When I feel shame as I sit in group, I*
> *lower my eyes and head.*

When you feel ashamed about sharing something with another person or a group, you may find yourself blushing, lowering your voice, or looking down and not wanting to look at others. You will begin to heal from your shame when you have the courage to identify and talk about it. In your recovery work, you come to realize that all human beings are pretty much the same and have done and felt many of the same things. A Twelve Step meeting is a good place to listen for the similarities and recognize that you are not alone. Your recovery will be greatly enhanced every time you choose to raise your head and talk about your secrets, instead of retreating into your inaccurate feelings of worthlessness.

Another important realization is:

> *When I encourage others to express their*
> *shame, it helps me to talk about mine.*

Learning to recognize the cues that other group members give about their own shame will further the healing that happens when chronic shame is exposed and talked about. You might say to a group member, "I notice you looked off and lowered your eyes when you talked about being yelled at. Are you feeling ashamed the way you used to when you were little?"

The more you can stand up to, gently face and expose your own and others' shame, the less power shame will have to rule your life, whether you learn to do and practice this in an adult children therapy group, a Twelve Step group, or in individual therapy.

Recognizing and Working through Grief

A significant part of your recovery work is grieving through your losses. This includes people, places, and things you've lost, as well as the things you "didn't get," such as a loving and supportive relationship with a parent or a childhood where having fun was expected and encouraged. Grief work also includes memories and concerns from the past and present, which might mean sharing painful memories of physical, verbal, or sexual abuse and talking about relationship losses, intimacy concerns, personal fears and insecurities, and fears of abandonment, anger, and losing control.

When you grieve, you can share your whole story and experience the healing of really being heard. The adult children in your group, your therapist, or sponsor will listen to you with their hearts.

A natural part of grief work involves healing memories in an experiential manner. Adult children are encouraged to "stay with their feelings" and to not try to "fix" each other. It is healing for someone to cry, to feel tears. It is also healing to release anger in a safe way. When old, bottled-up anger is released, it leaves room for new growth and insights. This natural grieving through expressing strong emotions is the central energizing, affirming, and healing part of the recovery experience.

Grief work occurs in phases and themes and these are not in any fixed order. No two adult children will proceed at the same pace. By trusting your intuition and the group process or the nudges you receive from your individual therapist or sponsor, you'll discover that you are developing and changing in the way and at the pace that is best for you.

An example of expressing grief is noticing:

Telling my whole story was a great relief.

To grieve over your past, it is important to let others know all about you. Taking your own time to tell your story and share your losses will begin your healing. There is no way that you can really grieve about your losses and move on without talking specifically about them. Every adult child in the recovery process deserves this opportunity, and there will be time for all to risk and share their past and present with each other.

Another important realization is:

*I learned that when grieving over my
losses I did not lose control of myself.*

Sometimes as you begin to grieve and tell your stories, you will be amazed at the power of the feelings that you have been keeping inside. You might want to hold back and stop your tears, sadness, and anger. Perhaps in your family, experiencing any emotions at all felt out of control, and the unspoken family rule was to either shut up or become violent. Beginning to feel intensely in a safe place is hard and important work. Expressing buried emotions may seem overwhelming at first, but this will moderate and become less intense over time.

Many adult children also feel:

> *I worry that there will never be an end to my grief.*

The journey through your sorrow, fear, and anger has an end. Accepting the reality of past losses is an important goal in your recovery work. Your first aim is self-forgiveness. You need to remember that you learned some maladaptive ways to cope and survive. It's time to forgive yourself, so you can move on and learn healthier ways of coping and relating. Your ability to forgive others will be easier when you come to the place in your own recovery where you are strong enough to step back and look more objectively at what life must have been like for your mother and father when *they* were children. You'll probably discover that, if they didn't meet your emotional needs, it was because of their own losses and lack of nurturing. As you understand their deprivation, it may be easier to offer them your forgiveness. Perhaps then you'll realize more fully that there was nothing wrong with you personally, that, instead, your experiences were the result of your parents' unmet needs and the emotional upheavals that accompany family dysfunction, especially the disease of addiction. If you choose to forgive them, it is important to do this when you are ready and to understand that you are forgiving them in order for you to let go of your own painful past.

Defining Personal Boundaries

The natural process of growing up is one of separation and individuation, of becoming your own person. But because of the disease process, emotions in alcoholic families are often enmeshed, and boundaries are blurred. Family members don't develop a sense of where, when, and how they need to be emotionally "separate" from each other. For example, some children in the alcoholic or otherwise dysfunctional family develop the role of being super-responsible and may become the family "caretakers." While growing up, adult children often felt some sense of safety, connection, and control from being emotionally "mixed together" with family members, but in adult relationships this is called "co-dependency" and is often crippling. When family members haven't learned to listen to their own needs, they will often experience feelings of fear and guilt as they begin to let go of old behaviors.

Defining your boundaries is a matter of drawing a line where you end and another person begins, of learning to be responsible **to** others, not **for** them. It is learning to allow others to have the privilege and responsibility of owning their own growth work. When you build your own boundaries, you not only become responsible **for** yourself, but **to** yourself as well. It includes grieving over the past, "letting go," and finding your own space and dignity in life. This personal freedom then allows you to choose how you wish to be involved with others.

An example of building a personal boundary is:

> *When I talk about how controlled I feel by*
> *my family and friends, I begin to under-*
> *stand how to set appropriate limits.*

Risking and telling your group, your therapist, or sponsor about the ways you let others take responsibility for you when you could do it yourself is an important part of recovery work. Learning to take in honest feedback about the appropriateness of what others do for you is the beginning of developing the objectivity necessary to change dependent behaviors. For example, if another group member tells you, "I think you expect your boyfriend to read your mind," you could respond, "I guess I do sometimes, because I was so good at it in my family, I expect everyone else to know what I think or feel without telling them."

When you get to a point in unhealthy relationships where you no longer are stuck in self-blame and you realize that others have unacceptable behaviors that they are unwilling to change, you may panic. This panic feels like a kick in the stomach, and you may feel unable to function, trapped in a sense of overwhelming helplessness. You're panicked because you realize you can't change them and, if you set new boundaries, they might not accept them. This often raises the ultimate fear of adult children—that others will abandon them or that they'll need to leave a relationship so they can continue to grow. As a child when you felt abandoned, you didn't have the resources to deal with your panic. As a resourceful adult, you need to recognize that this is an important turning point in your recovery. You now have the tools to grieve over your losses and ask for the support you need, as you set healthy boundaries for yourself and face your fears of abandonment.

Learning Missing Skills

When an adult child is having difficulty in some area of life, it is important to explore the possibility that a developmental skill is lacking. To put it simply: you can't do what you haven't been taught.

Social Skills

Many adult children have difficulty in friendships and other relationships because intimacy and healthy communication skills were not modeled effectively in childhood. Authors who write about the experience of adult children have referred to this phenomenon as a "recovery lag" or "missing database." During your adult child recovery work, use your group, therapist, or sponsor to help you identify, learn, and practice these missing developmental skills, especially in the areas of socializing and in maintaining relationships.

A way to develop social skills is to acknowledge:

> *I didn't learn how to relate to people*
> *when I was growing up because no one*
> *ever taught me.*

It is an important first step to recognize that there probably are social skills you missed learning. Then you can ask the questions you thought were too dumb to ask before: "How do I ask someone I like out?" or "What are some things to do on a first date?" When you were growing up, you may have felt ashamed and tried to pretend that you had all the answers in relationships.

It takes a lot of energy to keep pretending. Now you have a safe place to be honest, take off your mask, and learn the social skills you need to be successful.

Feelings Skills

To be able to talk about your feelings, it is necessary to learn what feelings are and how to identify them in yourself. Adult children express their lack of feelings skills by recognizing:

> *I couldn't talk about my feelings because fear or numbness was all I ever felt.*

or:

> *I know I'm supposed to be feeling something now, but I'm not, and I don't know how to begin to learn about feelings.*

You will find that many adult children haven't been taught to identify and express feelings. Your adult children therapy group will be a place to learn the language of feelings together. Perhaps in your family there was a lot of "mind reading" and guessing about what was going on, especially during times of tension and conflict. Your group will be the place to stop this mind-reading, to ask others what they are thinking and feeling, and to identify and share your own feelings. Taking this kind of risk will help you stop playing emotional guessing games and free your energies so you can be more available to yourself and others.

Conflict Resolution Skills

Members of alcoholic families and other families under stress often don't feel safe to express feelings directly and to challenge each other's behaviors. They are unwilling to share their honest reactions with each other and may develop "people pleasing" and excessive "caretaking" qualities to gain acceptance and mask their real feelings. An important part of recovery is learning to reverse this, to express your feelings directly to others, instead of denying and burying your reactions. Recovering people need to learn how to resolve conflict in a direct, honest, and caring manner.

In a therapy group, no one is permitted to attack another

member. Instead, members help themselves and each other grow by sharing their honest reactions. They are then better able to "step back," receive feedback, and see their behavior more objectively. The group is a microcosm of the real world; behaviors that occur in group often happen in our outside lives. In your relationship with an individual therapist or Twelve Step sponsor, it is just as important to share your honest feelings. You may feel your therapist or sponsor knows more because of his or her training or time in recovery, but the person best able to know you and how you are feeling is you. Challenging old behaviors in yourself and others will give you necessary information that can lead to recognizing options, making choices, and developing new, positive behaviors.

When we do not choose to be honest, we start putting distance between ourselves and others. As the distance grows, we begin to feel less safe, and as we feel less safe, we numb out. Does this sound familiar? It should. Remember, there are new rules in recovery. Risking is expected, wanted, and needed.

An example of healthy conflict resolution might be:

> *When I stood up for myself, I was scared*
> *she wouldn't like me.*

We fear telling others our true reactions because we have not learned the value and skill of honest, nonaggressive confrontation and communication. We tend to monitor our replies to ensure others will like us. But there is no magic formula that will guarantee that everyone will like us all the time. In fact, others respect us more when we are honest. You can learn how to be honestly confrontive without being verbally abusive. If you find yourself second-guessing your responses and talking a lot, it's a good clue that you may be avoiding being honest.

Another example of healthy confrontation is:

> *When I told the group leader he hurt my*
> *feelings, I was frightened about what his*
> *reaction would be.*

To tell a group leader, your individual therapist, or sponsor when you're feeling hurt or angry at him or her is like standing up to your mom or dad. It may not have been safe in your family to express your true feelings to your parents. To take a risk feels like standing alone and wondering if you'll be shamed or punished.

When you are upset or have something to say, it is important to be honest and say it. It is the responsibility of the group leader, your therapist, or sponsor to take care of himself /herself. It is important for you to trust that they will respond to you in appropriate ways. You have the right to "be heard" and treated with respect in all facets of your recovery program. If, after confronting an issue, you continue to feel unheard, it may be wise to review the situation with a trusted, objective person. In some cases, it may be appropriate to change your therapist, sponsor, and/or ACoA group. Please refer to Chapter One.

Affirmations

Giving yourself affirmations is a powerful skill that helps activate the healing energy of love. The daily practice of affirming your goodness, strengths, and positive expectations builds a fertile foundation for your ongoing growth. Writing, reading, and verbalizing these personalized affirmation statements will cause a powerful attitude change, as you come to realize that you are worthy of healing and happiness.

Some people feel that affirmations are great for everyone else, but not for them. But it has been demonstrated that five minutes of daily affirmation work will produce marked positive results in as little as one week. Concentrating on your affirmations and believing that they are true really will work for you. You need to create affirmations that feel right for you. It is important to keep them simple and in the present tense, as if they already were a reality.

Some examples are:

- *I am happy, relaxed, and peaceful.*
- *I am happy, content, and successful.*
- *I am intelligent, talented, and creative.*
- *I love myself and others abundantly.*
- *I am always in the right place at the right time, doing what is right for me.*

- *I have the resources to handle every situation successfully.*

- *I radiate happiness and love in all my relationships.*

- *Everything is working for good in my life.*

- *The light within me is guiding me in a perfect and right direction.*

- *I am perfectly protected and safe.*

Recognizing and Choosing Options

"Options" is a word that will be continually repeated in your recovery work. Adult children often felt constrained in making decisions when they were growing up. The ever shifting and unpredictable world of alcoholism didn't produce the safe and consistent climate needed to explore a range of choices. A child's choices were often made in response to current crises instead of his or her individual needs. You will find that through the process of embracing the past, acknowledging your old, unfinished business and grieving over your losses, a whole new world of options and choices naturally unfolds.

An example of exploring options is:

> *When I made a decision and realized I had a choice, I didn't feel so trapped anymore.*

It is easy to get locked into rigid patterns of behavior and response, especially with our families. Nothing will feel quite as freeing as the realization that it is loving and appropriate for you to make choices in your own best interest.

Perhaps you have always gone home for Thanksgiving and witnessed painful family battles that ruined your holiday. In your adult child recovery work, you will learn to explore options. Choosing not to go home for a disruptive holiday might be the wisest decision you can make. In learning to take better care of yourself, you will begin to realize that honesty and serenity are the best gifts you can give yourself and others. When you were little, you didn't have many choices, but now you will find that you are able to think through what is good for you and plan your life accordingly.

There are no perfect choices. You might have felt stuck in indecision in the past as you tried to make choices that would please everyone. Seldom is any choice perfectly clear or unanimously approved. You may have to settle for 51 percent in favor of a decision instead of 90 or 100 percent. You will learn that it is your willingness to be honest in making decisions that will give you a sense of peace and allow you to sleep well at night. It is also all right for you to make poor decisions; we all do at times. You know you're on the path of recovery when you view your poor decisions as lessons instead of mistakes.

Conclusion

Most adult children discover that a willingness to do this groundwork is vital to lasting recovery. You might find that you'll work on a couple of aspects at a time or work on one, leave it for a while, and then come back to it. There is no one right way to do your recovery work; you will address issues in your own time and style.

There is, however, a fairly consistent pattern of feelings that adult children experience as they move through recovery. While this pattern isn't rigid and absolute for all adult children, you'll find it easier to accept and grow through these feelings knowing that they are a normal part of the path of recovery. We'll talk about this path in the next chapter.

⚏ THREE ⚏

The Path of Recovery

This chapter explains some of the feelings adult children often experience in their recovery process. These same feelings may occur to a greater and lesser degree in all humans as they move through their natural life span and grieve through their losses, but we have found that some are more dominant for adult children. It is important to remember that this Path of Recovery is a guide, not a rigid and fixed timetable. Each person will experience feelings in his or her own way, but there seems to be a common healing path as adult children move from chronic shame through grief work into individuation and greater self-love.

It is important for adult children to see that grieving over their losses is a process they will progress through. Many have been fearful and reluctant to begin recovery for fear of getting lost and stuck in their hurt, fear, or anger. They often ask, "The past is over—why can't I just shut the door and forget it? Why open up a can of worms?" Adult children tell us years later that shutting the door didn't work. They often find themselves stuck in new pain-filled relationships and are unable to live balanced, healthy lives. When they did risk grieving and moving through the pain of the past, they found new freedom and happiness in their daily lives and relationships.

It is very helpful and inspiring for adult children to see the Path of Recovery as a way through and out of childhood pain, so we've included a diagram. We begin at the bottom of the path with chronic shame and work our way up to self-love and individuation. Chronic shame feeds our sense of fear, anger, and powerlessness that is often expressed inappropriately as either depression or rage, which in turn makes us feel more shame. But, along the Path of Recovery we can choose to move out of rage and depression and try more hopeful new behaviors.

The Healing Process

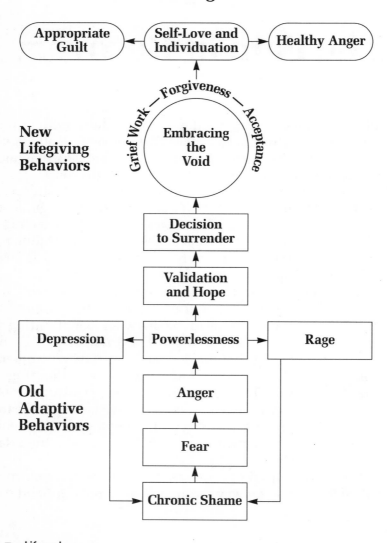

With hope and validation, we can find the willingness to surrender and embrace the void, where we learn to grieve, forgive, accept, and love ourselves. As we become more fully ourselves through individuation, we learn to feel appropriate guilt and express anger in healthy, affirming ways. We heal. We become whole. It is important to keep the whole journey in mind as we move along the path, particularly when we fear the next step.

Chronic Shame

Chronic shame feelings develop in our childhood and form the core of low self-worth that extends its tentacles into depression and anxiety. This core feeling radiates a deep sense of worthlessness. When our shame surfaces, we often feel inadequate and "less than" others. Deep shame feels intolerable. Human beings struggle to escape the sense of degradation that accompanies shame.

As explained in Chapter Two, chronic shame is paralyzing in a way that guilt or healthy shame is not. Chronic shame is feeling "I am a mistake" instead of "I made a mistake." Denied and buried feelings of shame often block the healthy release of anger and expressions of hurt. We begin our healing path of recovery by being willing to tap into our shame core. Accepting that our shame is real, and being willing to look at its effects in our life, is the beginning of our journey into self-knowledge and healing.

Signs of shame might include:

- feeling uncomfortable with the opposite sex, but pretending not to be

- feeling shame about our bodies and, as a result, hiding under layers of clothes

- missing events and avoiding relationships in which we feel we'd be physically exposed

- having difficulty maintaining eye contact when we are talking to someone

- feeling terrified that we are so bad that if people "really" knew us, they'd reject us

- feeling so much panic that we sometimes avoid situations by spacing out, not paying attention, leaving the room, or actually running out

- feeling such disgust and revulsion about a mistake we've made that we become emotionally and physically ill and unable to forgive ourselves the way we could a friend who had done the exact same thing
- avoiding mirrors or not looking directly into them
- having difficulty asking for help because we feel we might inconvenience someone.

Fear

Chronic shame plants seeds of inadequacy in our self-esteem. Shame causes us to doubt our self-worth and wonder if we really are good people. Self-doubt and feelings of shame-based inadequacy cause us to feel great waves of fear in encountering many living and relationship situations. We seem to always wonder if we will be "good enough." We feel like impostors in our own lives and so we expend great amounts of energy to "put on a good front." Our ungrounded fear is that our mask will slip away and our inadequacy will be exposed to others. Control in many forms is employed to cover shame-based fears.

Some signs of bondage to fear include fearing that:

- we are on the verge of losing control
- we'll be laughed at if we express strong feelings
- no matter what we do, we feel we won't fit in
- we are so confused, we don't know who we are—this perhaps includes prolonged concerns about our sexual identity.

We may attempt to control the fear by:

- overplanning, overeating, overdrinking, etc....
- rushing
- being obsessed with details and trying to figure out what the panic means
- getting sick to avoid a fearful person or situation
- isolating ourselves.

Initial Anger

Our continued efforts to control our shame-based feelings of inadequacy are exhausting and time-consuming. We try to hide our true feelings behind masks, but feelings cannot be hidden and denied indefinitely. They will always surface in one way or another, and sooner or later our natural anger emerges, often in inappropriate outbursts.

In most dysfunctional families, anger has not been modeled in direct and appropriate ways. Since we are locked in shame and fear, our anger will reflect our self-doubt and efforts at emotional control. Initial anger may frighten us with the power of its bottled-up intensity. We may kick the dog or yell at a boyfriend for no real reason. Extreme guilt and confusion usually follows such outbursts. These inappropriate behaviors add to our stockpile of chronic shame and make us feel powerless to honestly know and express our real feelings in appropriate ways.

Examples of expressing anger inappropriately are:

- finding "reasons" for not showing up for group or other appointments

- being chronically late

- getting irritated with everything others say and do after an upsetting phone call from a parent

- feeling upset because, no matter how hard we study or work at our jobs, we feel we could do better

- being upset with a spouse or partner for not meeting all our needs

- being afraid to get angry because we're afraid we'll lose control

- abusing food, alcohol, or some other numbing substance or process

- overspending on items we don't really need

- feeling as if our predominant feelings are sadness, loneliness, and sometimes self-pity

- being overly nice, sweet, and compliant

- expressing rage that is too intense to fit the situation at authority figures, clerks, public officials, police officers, and others.

Powerlessness

Powerlessness is a feeling that occurs when a person feels "stuck" in pain and old behaviors. Shame, fear, and misdirected anger create a harmful cycle that the adult child feels can't be controlled. No matter how much effort is made, there still remains a deep feeling of dissatisfaction and uselessness. Since relationships seem especially affected, adult children at this point on the path often feel powerless to be in a healthy relationship for any period of time. A sense of shame, inadequacy, fear, and misdirected anger will exhaust them and create an attitude of helplessness.

Powerlessness may be found in:

- our inability to make decisions
- perfectionism
- asking for help, but always rejecting or finding fault with the suggestions offered
- neglecting personal hygiene and exercise
- having overly critical attitudes about others
- switching jobs and vocational plans
- over-enmeshment with Mom and Dad
- always failing just before meeting a goal
- finding something seriously displeasing in most people.

Depression and Rage

Depression and rage demonstrate different sides of the same coin. Powerlessness and its chronic shame base are intolerable human feelings. Sooner or later they will need to erupt in anger against ourselves (depression) or anger against others (rage). Rage and depression act out our unresolved feeling life in hurtful and unfulfilling ways. Rage and long-term depressions are nonproductive. Eventually they may contribute to obsessions, compulsions, and addictions that circle back and add to our stockpile of chronic shame.

Chronic shame then reactivates the same painful feeling process. This shame merry-go-round can continue for years unless this pattern is changed. Growing up in our alcoholic or dysfunctional family, we may have survived and adapted to the pain by staying in a chronic shame cycle. Perhaps no one taught us how to express our feelings honestly and directly or, when we did, we may have been shamed or abused for disrupting the family system. These old adaptive behaviors may have been the safest or only way we had to survive, but now as adults we find our old behaviors cause us pain and aren't healthy for us.

Recovery begins with a small degree of willingness to try out new life behaviors. As we move out of the rage and depression phase of the shame cycle, we are given a choice to journey upward on our path of recovery. We can decide to reach up to hope or revert back down into pain.

Signs of depression, the **internalization** of shame, hurt, fear, powerlessness, and unresolved anger, include:

- being afraid to take the risks of getting to know others

- having no energy

- struggling to remember the last time we had fun, or imagining what it would feel like to enjoy what we are doing

- engaging in constant self-criticism or abusive self-talk

- experiencing many physical symptoms, such as changes in sleeping and eating patterns

- feeling suicidal.

Signs of rage, the **externalization** of shame, hurt, fear, powerlessness, and unresolved anger include:

- criticizing or verbally abusing someone else

- vicious gossip or put downs about others

- driving after drinking

- chronic lying
- physically hurting ourselves or others
- smiling when we feel angry
- sexually abusing ourselves (promiscuity, chronic masturbation, etc.) or others.

Hope

Hope is a spark that grows in warmth and brightness as we begin to believe that we can heal some of our past hurts. This spark of hope is often fanned by the growth we see in others in our adult children therapy group as they heal. As we are willing to read about and listen to the struggles and victories of other adult children, a voice inside us says, "Yes, I can feel better if I am willing to open up and risk telling people about myself." Nurturing this hopeful feeling is a courageous step that allows us to be open and vulnerable to the process of change.

Risk-taking increases our hope. Each time we decide to take a risk and be open in honestly sharing our feelings and reactions, we experience more hope. Hope is built by standing up and making choices about our life that we feel are right for us. Hope is a growing willingness to believe that our judgment can be correct and that we can trust others for honest feedback as we try out new risk-taking behaviors. Hope is choosing to believe in your own resources to make choices regarding your life.

Hope can be expressed by making a choice to:

- not go home for a holiday
- date someone my friend doesn't like
- study in a field or take a job because it will make me happy even though my parents or others disapprove
- ask the group to let me sit back and not participate when I feel unable to share
- take up as much group time as I need to tell my whole story
- cry about the shame and embarrassment I feel about my mom's drinking

- keep coming back to counseling when I am feeling powerful feelings

- believe others who say that my life will get better if I am willing to be honest and open.

Validation

Validation is learning to accept our gifts, goodness, and worth. When we hear good things about ourselves, we may want to turn away and reject the compliments. We may be unwilling to affirm our good qualities and positive feelings. Adult children are often experts in self-criticism and personal fault-finding. Negativity may be an old companion that says: "I'll put myself down before you do" or "If I acknowledged my worth, what would happen when I didn't do well? Would I get rejected as I did when I was little? Maybe I'll keep rejecting myself first, so I'll be expecting the pain and it won't hurt so much."

As we learn to stop criticizing ourselves and savor validation, we fill up with a healthy surge of power. Thoughts like: "Yes, maybe I *am* good" begin to bounce around inside us. Adult children are starved for the healing tonic of validation that can soothe years of shame feelings. We can begin to offer ourselves validating messages as a statement of our commitment to a healthy life.

Validating thoughts and comments include:

- Even though this relationship didn't work out, I'm glad I took the risk in getting to know him.

- I was initially afraid of my father's reaction, but I'm glad I talked to him about my feelings.

- I'm starting to accept compliments from others and risk believing they're true.

- I'm starting to be less judgmental of myself even though my body isn't magazine picture perfect.

- This week for the first time I was able to accept that getting a "B" doesn't mean I'm a failure as a student.

- I realize that everybody doesn't have to like me for me to be okay.
- The money and time I spend in therapy is an important investment in my own life.

The Decision to Surrender

We make a decision to surrender when we choose to walk through our pain, instead of running away from it. When we were little children, we needed to hold tight to our reins of control in order to stay safe in our families. We may never have cried because mom or dad would have mocked our tears. We may have kept all of our feelings secret because expressed feelings were ignored or blown out of proportion in our families. We may have hid in books, eaten cookies, or sat quietly in corners, so as not to add to the upsets in our day-to-day living.

Now we are different. We have resources to take care of ourselves that we didn't have in our first family. We can surrender some of our old pain and protective ways of behaving and explore new healing options. We can let go of the belief that we always have to be in control. As we learn to take risks and be open to the feedback of others who care about us, we are able to surrender ourselves to the healing process. Surrender is a choice to open ourselves and walk through the fears, angers and hurts that we previously ran away from. Our surrender marks our decision to embrace our uncharted places and to get to know ourselves as we really are, trusting that we will have the resources to meet and tame our personal monsters.

Surrender may be experienced when we:

- get honest in group about what we are experiencing underneath our silence
- put our anger aside and try to hear the caring feedback of others regarding our behavior
- let ourselves cry without trying to stop the tears
- are willing to "sit with" uncomfortable feelings, trusting they will pass
- stay in a loving relationship and work through the rough times instead of running away.

Embracing the Void

As we journey into the deepest parts of ourselves, we encounter our grandest gifts and our greatest dreads. To feel abandoned and alone is a child's worst nightmare. As children who didn't feel safe, we often built defensive walls to protect us and make us feel less alone. Now as adults we are ready to take down the walls that have kept us from really knowing ourselves and others. We are now challenged to be vulnerable, to identify and talk about our feelings without trying to run away or cover them up. The inner void is the part of us that isn't used to being exposed. We may feel "abandonment anxiety" or a feeling of almost total vulnerability. As we choose to trust and take leaps of honesty, we wonder if there will be a net to catch us if we fall. We dread abandonment feelings and often believe they are intolerable. We may be tempted to return to old, hurtful relationships or behaviors as a way to temporarily alleviate the pain.

Adult children with strong, paralyzing fears of abandonment are often victims of unresolved and ungrieved for childhood shaming experiences. Sooner or later we are all challenged to make the most important journey back to the frightened little child inside of us. Until we meet, comfort, and sit with that child, we will be afraid of life and its necessary times of solitude and loss. Abandonment anxiety will not kill us—it just feels that way at times. Working through this anxiety is embracing the void.

It may take awhile before we are able to identify and express these deep fears and hurts. With continuing effort, we will be able to link our current feelings with childhood hurts. As we acknowledge, mourn, and let go of our childhood losses, we are better equipped to separate old relationship pains from our present lives. We will find that the present becomes more manageable when it is untangled from the web of yesterday's sorrow and grief.

Once we adult children confront our inner void and work through the dread of abandonment anxiety, we will never feel it with the same force again. A remarkable thing happens as abandonment issues are worked through: we become more capable of being present in our own lives. The experience of facing what we dread most and surviving it is life-giving and freeing.

We can embrace the void when we:

- don't change the subject when we feel afraid to talk

- leave a harmful relationship and work through the pain of the loss instead of returning

- let ourselves experience and work through the guilt of saying no to someone

- move to a new place, where we don't know anyone

- cry, instead of laughing and pretending we don't hurt

- ask for help and support from someone else.

Grief Work

Grief work weaves itself in and out of our path of recovery. When we do our grief work, we accept our losses as real and allow ourselves to feel all of our emotions about these losses. We move toward resolving our shame, pain, anger, and fear by acknowledging and sharing these feelings with others who are safe.

Grief is an integral part of all vital living. We may have had a tendency to connect grief only with the loss of someone through death, but more and more we are coming to recognize that grief is experienced almost anytime we lose something of value, whether the loss is great or small. Adult children need to grieve over the losses of significant relationships in which they had come to expect love and care. Relationship griefs are often the seeds of our deepest pain and we yearn to be able to talk and cry about them, to express them completely. Losses often pile up and contain months and years of broken dreams. We find that we gain a new-found sense of peace and a boost in self-esteem when we share and grieve over our personal stories. Initially we may be shocked by the power of our buried feelings, but our surprise is overshadowed by feelings of relief and gratitude as we unburden ourselves.

When we grieve, we recognize that:

- when we tell our own story, we are grieving

- healing is a process that takes time
- endings bring new beginnings
- some losses are necessary in order to move on in our lives
- we have the tools to choose among many options
- we are challenged to befriend and own our feelings
- it is necessary to let go of some dreams
- each person has his/her own unique way of grieving over losses
- there is no right or wrong way to grieve.

Forgiveness

Forgiveness is the willingness to let go of resentments and our desire to punish ourselves or others. Sometimes adult children stay connected to others through negativity and pain. Many of us feel that we're unable to forgive someone who has hurt us deeply. We ask, "How can I consider forgiving my father? I can never forget how much he hurt me." Or, "Forgive her? That would be like saying her actions were all right."

Some adult children find that forgiveness is not a present part of their healing path. To forgive or not to forgive is an individual choice and needs to be respected as such. It is primarily a gift of unburdening that we may choose to give ourselves. It may take time and occur in little pieces, but it is helpful for all adult children to find ways to let go of the negative strings that tie them to their past.

We need to recognize that, when we forgive, we don't have to forget the pain that is a part of our history. In fact, we can't forgive what we don't remember. We can choose to remember without reliving, rethinking, and re-feeling our old pain and anger. We also need to recognize that the primary motive for forgiveness is loving self-interest. We limit our freedom when we use our energy to carry negative feelings around. Reliving old hurts and resentments weighs us down; releasing them lightens our load.

When we forgive, we recognize that:

- the most important persons to forgive and accept are ourselves
- we no longer need to stay emotionally connected to others through anger and pain
- we have the ability to take care of ourselves by setting new limits in relationships
- forgiving is not necessarily forgetting.

Acceptance

We reach acceptance when we are able to acknowledge and grieve over the reality of our past experiences while focusing on changing our own attitudes, instead of denying the past and trying to change other people, places, and things. Acceptance deepens the healing of shame-based judgments of ourselves. When we accept, we grieve over our losses, then pick up the pieces of our lives as gifts to be treasured and built upon.

When we accept, we recognize that:

- we are capable of asking others to meet needs that were not met in our families
- we can't change others
- life isn't always fair
- we don't always get what we want
- when one door closes, another will open
- we have personal power to make a difference in our lives
- when we stop comparing ourselves, we can begin to appreciate our own and others' uniqueness
- yesterday is gone and today is our treasure chest.

Self-love

Self-love is the visible and invisible expression of our self-esteem. Adult children demonstrate self-love when they are willing to care for their own physical, emotional, and spiritual needs as a priority in their lives. Self-love is demonstrated when we can say no to demands that are not good for us. Adult children often put their own needs last and feel it's selfish to put their needs first. But, as our awareness of our goodness and value as human beings grows, we are able to value ourselves appropriately. This is the opposite of being selfish. As we learn to be more honest, we find that we can't effectively give to others unless we first nurture and give to ourselves.

When we love ourselves we recognize that:

- we are balanced human beings and need to respect our physical, emotional, and spiritual needs
- it is essential to say no when the demands of others exceed our limits
- we have the right to make mistakes and change our minds
- we have the right to be respected.

Individuation

Adult children often get entangled in the lives of others, as we try to fit our lives into a confused, changing world. We may have become experts in "mind and situation reading," learning to anticipate the emotional climates in relationships. When we over-focused on others, we didn't have the time or energy to decide what our own feelings and reactions were. As we follow the path of recovery, we learn to individuate ourselves, that is, to separate ourselves from enmeshed relationships, establish personal boundaries, and recognize ourselves as unique and valuable human beings. We individuate ourselves by getting to know who we really are and what we truly value. When we find out what we believe in, we are better able to stand up to others and honestly express our needs and differences. Today, we feel proud of our emerging ability to recognize ourselves as separate from others. Our lives become more peaceful and less complicated when we are able to express our individuality.

We individuate ourselves when we:

- set boundaries, make choices, and assert what we want

- are safely separate from others

- distinguish between being interdependent and independent

- recognize that getting to know ourselves is a process of discovering our uniqueness

- take the time to make ourselves a priority and do what we need to do to take care of ourselves

- allow others the privilege of making their own mistakes and living their own lives.

Appropriate Guilt

As we grow in our recovery, we find that our chronic shame is replaced with feeling guilt when it is appropriate for us to do so. Guilt and nonchronic shame feelings are markers of our sense of human responsibility to ourselves and others. We are not perfect, and we will occasionally make poor judgments and do things that hurt others. Appropriate guilt reminds us of our responsibility to be accountable for our actions. Instead of sinking into the mire of chronic shame, we can choose to acknowledge our unloving or hurtful actions. We can be willing to take responsibility for our actions and choose to make more loving decisions in the future. Acknowledging appropriate guilt frees us from relationship tangles.

Appropriate guilt is expressed when we:

- say we're sorry when we hurt someone and try to act differently next time

- sort out what we are and are not accountable for

- stop judging ourselves harshly for our poor judgments

- focus more on our value and gifts than on our negative aspects.

Healthy Anger

Along the path of recovery, we find that healthy anger replaces rage and depression just as appropriate guilt replaces chronic shame. When we were caught in the shame cycle, we may have automatically reacted with rage or depression as a form of self-protection. We didn't know how to address the depression that was the result of burying our anger or expressing it indirectly, and it turned into outbursts of rage that destroyed relationships. Rage and depression imprisoned us; we didn't have the tools or insight that would have freed us to express anger in healthy ways.

We are learning that anger is a necessary and healing part of life and grieving over the inevitable losses we all face. It is natural for us to feel and express anger when we feel devalued or hurt. Through our grief work on the path of recovery, we are now able to stop and choose before we act. We are able to respond in more loving ways to ourselves and others; we can express anger suitably, assertively sharing our strong feelings without attacking.

Anger can be our friend and a relationship barometer. We can choose to use it directly and honestly. It is a gift to show others our true selves. When they feel safe with us, it opens rich possibilities of love and communication. We discover new freedom and intimacy with ourselves and others.

We express healthy anger when we:

- choose safe people and safe places to express our pain, losses, and anger about all we didn't get while growing up in our families

- believe that assertively expressing our anger is beneficial and doesn't mean we are crazy or out of control; that, in fact, choosing when and with whom to get angry comes from a position of real personal power instead of merely reacting

- find that our friends like the fact that we're more direct with our feelings because they know where we stand.

No matter where on this path you start the process of recovery or how hard you work, life's circumstances will inevitably influence your pace. Be gentle with yourself. Do not judge yourself harshly if you find that some tasks and feelings are more difficult to face than others. Remember that you have many adaptive survival skills that are hard to let go of because they aided you in the past by providing you a degree of comfort and allowing you to know what to expect. As you focus on recovery, you are beginning to explore uncharted territory. Using Chapter Four, "Personal Lifework," provides you with a structure to begin exploring your past and the impact it's had on you as well as laying a foundation for recovery. You do not have to be alone on this journey anymore.

⌑ FOUR ⌑

Personal Lifework

Recovery requires a journey into your past. Healing begins with the first step you take into personal discovery. By remembering and retelling your personal history, you will be empowered to discover the source of old feelings and painful memories that negatively affect your life today.

Along this recovery journey you will review your gifts and strengths, along with the pain and difficulties of your childhood. You will recall both good and bad memories, and realize that you have known both healing and hurtful relationships.

Alcoholism and other chronic illnesses and family dysfunctions often cause the children in a family a great deal of pain and confusion in childhood and in their passage to adolescence and adulthood. But alcohol is not the only culprit to be acknowledged in the following pages of *Lifework*. Alcohol and its effects on families are only some of the pieces in a puzzle that contains numerous life issues that are faced by all humans as they grow up. Many of your experiences are not unique to adult children, but can be found in a range of families.

As you explore your personal history in the light of today's reality, you will begin to experience a new freedom, born of your willingness to take risks and share your vulnerability with your group or therapist. Be assured that when your individual pain, joy, fear, hope, anger, love, hurt, and shame are expressed, one underlying truth will emerge: every human being is worthwhile and deserves respect. Accepting and valuing this goodness in yourself and others is the true work of your therapy experience.

Recovery is the process of making friends with yourself. It is coming to terms with your personal monsters by turning to face them. Your fears and problems can become manageable when you acknowledge and share them with others. The recovery experience is a stepping stone backward into your past and then forward into your daily life where the real work and learning is done.

To help you keep track of this work and learning you're doing along your Path of Recovery, this section of *Lifework* is divided into three sections: Family History, Feelings Reflections, and Reflections Journal.

Your responses here should be free-flowing and seen as lifework, not homework. As you write (or draw) in each of these sections, forget all the rules you learned about "correct writing." Don't worry about spelling. Forget about margins, perfect penmanship, and proportion. Draw stick figures, and add whatever details are significant to you. Write incomplete sentences if you need to in order to keep up with your thoughts and feelings.

Keep in mind that this journal is for you. Anyone you choose to share it with is going to be interested in the emotion you reveal and the growth you experience, not the grammar and style.

Family History

This section provides exercises to help you explore and retell your family history. In the process of understanding your place in your family of origin, it is important to be flexible. Aim to see yourself at different times and in different roles. We are all developmentally unique, and we pass in and out of many phases and roles during our lifetimes.

Overall, defining which roles you played is probably not as important as discovering your behavioral patterns and themes. Keep in mind that family members develop adaptive behavioral responses to relieve stress and survive the best they can. Descriptions of general behavioral themes and questions that reveal the significance these patterns have in your life are at the end of this Family History section.

Feelings Reflections

This section asks questions about each of the feelings stages on the Path of Recovery. You can work through these questions sequentially, recording your responses to each question as it appears in the book, or you can select feelings that seem particularly relevant to you at a given time. Your group leader, therapist, or sponsor might, for example, suggest that you seem to be working on initial anger and rage issues or that you could benefit by considering hope or validation. Responding to the corresponding questions might be valuable to you at those times.

Reflections Journal

At first glance you might think this last section is just a collection of blank pages. Nevertheless it is a vital part of your *Lifework* workbook. It is a place to record your reactions to the other parts of this book, as well as to people, places, and things you notice during the week.

If you can't think of a thing to say, think about what your "personal nudges" were. What made you feel happy, sad, or mad? Where did you feel stuck? What did you bring from your last group or individual session into the week? How did you allow your gifts and strengths to work for you this week? What happened this week? What will you share with the group, your therapist, or your sponsor? What are you afraid to share?

Family History

Family Picture

Draw a spontaneous picture of your family of origin. Use a circle to represent each person, placing each circle in the same emotional and physical position you saw that family member in when you were a child. Make the sizes and spaces fit your memory as well as you can. There is no right or wrong way. Trust your first reactions in making your picture.

Reactions to Family Drawing

After you've finished your drawing, study it and record your emotional reactions to it. Include how you see yourself and your relationships with other family members. You may want to bring this picture to therapy or group to share as a way of letting others get to know you better.

_____

_____

_____

_____

_____

_____

_____

_____

_____

_____

Family Home

Draw a picture of your family home.

Close your eyes, take a few deep breaths, and imagine yourself walking through the front door and into each room. Record the feelings and reactions you experience. Write about the room you liked best and why. Write about the room you liked least and why. Who was in each room? Where were you? What were your reactions to the people in your home?

Family Relationships

List each family member and write a few spontaneous sentences about your past and current relationship with each person.

Who were you closest to, and why?

Who were you afraid of, and why?

Family Losses

What are some of the losses you experienced as a child? Be sure to include things you didn't get. Which of these losses have you grieved over? How did you grieve over them?

Unfinished Family Business

What unfinished business do you have with other family members? With whom do you have this unfinished business, and why? How is this affecting your life today?

Behavioral Themes

It is helpful to discover some of the behavioral themes you may have used to adapt and survive in your family, but remember there are no rigidly fixed family roles. You probably acted out several themes and may continue to switch back and forth over time.

Some common themes in dysfunctional families include:

Fixer	Does everything for others and often ignores personal needs
Isolator	Retreats and focuses energy on personal survival
Blamer	Uses energy to focus on and blame others and rarely acknowledges personal pain
Mind reader	Senses the emotional climate of the family and responds accordingly
Joker	Makes a lot of jokes or causes mischief to divert family pain and attention
Escape artist	Avoids the family whenever possible
Magician	Pretends that everything is okay
Child-Parent	Takes over the emotional or physical responsibilities of the parent(s)
Superachiever	Seeks self-esteem through excellence in accomplishments
Trouble-maker	Seeks attention through negative behaviors
Cloud	Moves in and out: "Now you see me, now you don't."

What behavioral themes did you use in your family?

_____

_____

_____

_____

_____

_____

_____

_____

_____

_____

_____

_____

_____

List the themes you learned. How do they positively and negatively affect your life today in areas such as relationships, self-esteem, sexuality, work, study, play, spirituality?

_____

_____

_____

_____

_____

_____

_____

_____

_____

_____

_____

_____

_____

What positive aspects of your behavior do you want to enhance and keep?

What nonproductive behaviors would you like to change?

_____

_____

_____

_____

_____

_____

_____

_____

_____

_____

_____

_____

What is your resistance to change? What might you "lose" or have to give up if you change?

Personal Change Plan

List specific actions you want to take in the future.

_____

_____

_____

_____

_____

_____

_____

_____

_____

_____

_____

_____

_____

Inventory of Strengths and Gifts

What strengths, gifts, and good memories do you bring from your childhood?

_____

_____

_____

_____

_____

_____

_____

_____

_____

_____

_____

_____

_____

_____

Feelings Reflections

The Healing Process

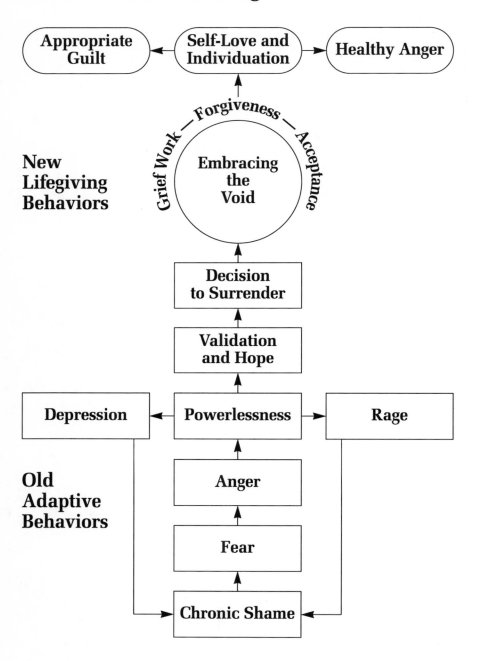

Chronic Shame

How and when have you have felt unhealthy, chronic shame?

_____

_____

_____

_____

_____

_____

_____

_____

_____

_____

_____

_____

_____

_____

When you were a child, what did you feel ashamed of?

What were the specific ways you felt ashamed of your family?

What were the ways you felt ashamed of your body?

_____

_____

_____

_____

_____

_____

_____

_____

_____

_____

_____

_____

What, if any, shameful secrets still haunt you?

Ongoing Shame Inventory

As you come to know yourself better, you will notice areas in your life where you experience self-judgment or chronic shame feelings. You can use these pages to date and jot down these important feelings when you notice them. Sharing these feelings with your therapist, your sponsor, or in the group will contribute to your growth.

Fear

What were your biggest childhood fears? Be as specific as possible.

_____

_____

_____

_____

_____

_____

_____

_____

_____

_____

_____

_____

_____

What childhood fears do you still carry today?

In what ways did your chronic shame feelings contribute to your fears?

_____

_____

_____

_____

_____

_____

_____

_____

_____

_____

_____

_____

_____

_____

Initial Anger

When you were a child, how did you express your anger or temper?

_____

_____

_____

_____

_____

_____

_____

_____

_____

_____

_____

_____

_____

What hurts preceded your anger?

_____

_____

_____

_____

_____

_____

_____

_____

_____

_____

_____

_____

_____

What role did anger play in your life as a child?

Did you learn to overexpress or underexpress your anger?
(Explain)

_____

_____

_____

_____

_____

_____

_____

_____

_____

_____

_____

_____

_____

How specifically did your parents and other family members express anger?

What childhood angers and expressions of anger do you still carry today?

_____

_____

_____

_____

_____

_____

_____

_____

_____

_____

_____

_____

_____

_____

Powerlessness

When you were a child, what circumstances made you feel powerless?

_____

_____

_____

_____

_____

_____

_____

_____

_____

_____

_____

_____

_____

What childhood feelings of powerlessness do you still carry today?

_____

_____

_____

_____

_____

_____

_____

_____

_____

_____

_____

_____

_____

Rage

In what ways have you raged against others?

_____

_____

_____

_____

_____

_____

_____

_____

_____

_____

_____

_____

_____

_____

How has your rage affected others?

How have you raged against yourself? How has your rage affected your body, mind, and spirit?

Depression

How and when have you been depressed? Include your earliest memories of depression and feelings of prolonged hopelessness and guilt.

_____

_____

_____

_____

_____

_____

_____

_____

_____

_____

_____

_____

What parts of your childhood depression do you still carry today?

Hope

How and when have you felt hope in your life before?

_____

_____

_____

_____

_____

_____

_____

_____

_____

_____

_____

_____

_____

What allows you to be hopeful today? Be specific.

Validation

In what ways do others validate you?

_____

_____

_____

_____

_____

_____

_____

_____

_____

_____

_____

_____

_____

_____

In what ways do you validate yourself?

Decision to Surrender

In what ways can you now "let go" and trust others?

_____

_____

_____

_____

_____

_____

_____

_____

_____

_____

_____

_____

What gets in the way of your willingness to surrender and trust that you will be healed?

Embracing the Void

What aspects of your true self are you afraid to know?

Why are you frightened to express your true feelings and let go of old pain and self-defeating behaviors?

_____

_____

_____

_____

_____

_____

_____

_____

_____

_____

_____

_____

_____

_____

When you think about "being alone with yourself," do you feel anxious, afraid, or abandoned? (Explain)

_____

_____

_____

_____

_____

_____

_____

_____

_____

_____

_____

_____

_____

Grief Work

What are the greatest losses in your life? Be sure to consider the things you didn't get.

Which losses do you find the hardest to grieve over and let go?

_____

_____

_____

_____

_____

_____

_____

_____

_____

_____

_____

_____

_____

Forgiveness

What anger, resentment, grudges, and hurt feelings are you holding on to?

_____

_____

_____

_____

_____

_____

_____

_____

_____

_____

_____

_____

_____

List whom and what you are ready to forgive.

_____

_____

_____

_____

_____

_____

_____

_____

_____

_____

_____

_____

_____

List whom and what you are **not** ready to forgive.

How, specifically, does your unwillingness or inability to forgive affect your own life?

How can you minimize the negative effects that come from this unwillingness or inability to forgive?

In what ways can you offer yourself the gift of forgiveness?

_____

_____

_____

_____

_____

_____

_____

_____

_____

_____

_____

_____

Acceptance

In what ways do you accept and care for yourself?

_____

_____

_____

_____

_____

_____

_____

_____

_____

_____

_____

_____

Self-Love

List all the things about yourself that you or others consider loveable.

_____

_____

_____

_____

_____

_____

_____

_____

_____

_____

_____

_____

_____

Individuation

In what ways and in which areas of your life are you learning to set boundaries and put your needs first?

_____

_____

_____

_____

_____

_____

_____

_____

_____

_____

_____

_____

_____

In what areas do you have a difficult time caring for yourself?

Whom do you have difficulty setting limits with? In what circumstances?

It is often easy when you grow up in an enmeshed family system to focus more on others' needs, thoughts, and feelings than your own. What are some specific ways you can stay focused on your own needs, thoughts, and feelings?

Appropriate Guilt

How do you recognize appropriate guilt and differentiate it from chronic shame?

In what ways are you learning to be accountable? Whom are you learning to be accountable to?

_____

_____

_____

_____

_____

_____

_____

_____

_____

_____

_____

_____

_____

Healthy Anger

Who and what makes you mad today?

_____

_____

_____

_____

_____

_____

_____

_____

_____

_____

_____

_____

_____

_____

How do you express anger in healthy ways?

It takes a great deal of courage to get to know our real selves. In recording your responses in these sections of *Lifework*, you have bravely taken your memories and feelings down from the shelves of your past to examine and expose them to the healing light of today.

We hope that you will respect and measure your recovery without comparing yourself to others. We are all different and recovery is a process that evolves over time. You are exactly where you need to be in your own growth work at this time. We validate the courage you have shown in doing your "lifework" and welcome you to the next chapter, Aftercare Planning. Use it to remind yourself of your current plans to take excellent care of yourself.

Remember, you are a treasure worthy of being loved and cherished.

Reflections Journal

▣ FIVE ▣

Aftercare Planning

The end of therapy does not typically mark a magic moment when you are totally transformed, but instills a sense that you've done some important grief work, learned some effective strategies for expressing your feelings, are more successful in your interactions with others, and now better understand how the past impacts the present. Now that you are at the end of your therapy experience, it is important to remember where you started and acknowledge the progress you've made. The following questions will help you and your therapist develop an aftercare plan for you.

Aftercare plans are roadmaps you can use as you journey into each new day of recovery. Trust the aftercare recommendations you and your therapist develop, even if they seem like a lot of work. Without direction, structure, and plans you may slip back into your old ways of reacting. The more you value and follow your aftercare plans, the greater your ongoing recovery benefits will be.

1. Describe yourself at the beginning of the adult child therapy process.

_____

_____

_____

_____

_____

2. What initial fears did you have about changing?

_____

_____

_____

_____

_____

3. When you were in a great deal of pain, what allowed you to trust the process enough to continue working in therapy?

_____

_____

_____

_____

4. What are the three most important recognitions or changes you made in this therapy process?

5. How can you use these new awarenesses and experiences to help you in your life now?

6. Record all aftercare recommendations made by your therapist.

7.	What specific things are you willing to commit to doing each week to aid you in continuing your recovery process?

_____

_____

_____

_____

_____

8.	Brainstorm anything you imagine might interfere or sabotage your aftercare plans.

_____

_____

_____

_____

9.	Which one of your personality traits may divert you from staying committed to aftercare?

_____

_____

_____

_____

10. If you feel stuck in your recovery in the future, what resources and strengths can you call on to support you?

_____

_____

_____

_____

11. How would you recognize the need to recommit to your aftercare plans? Write a specific plan for how you would reaffirm your commitment.

_____

_____

_____

_____

12. Identify your support systems and specify how you will use them.

_____

_____

_____

_____

⌘ APPENDIX ⌘

To the Therapist

Our hope is that you'll find *Lifework* a helpful tool in your work with clients who grew up in alcoholic or other dysfunctional families. Since this book was written reflecting our belief that an adult children therapy group provides a comprehensive treatment approach, the material and examples assume the client is participating in this kind of group. If you are facilitating a group of adult children, *Lifework* can provide direction and help you manage the enormous grief issues that present themselves with this population. We hope you'll use this workbook as a guide; feel free to be flexible and use the sections you believe are appropriate to your group.

 Lifework provides a starting place for an adult child to begin the important journey of recovery. Each client and therapy group will have its own unique character and will respond differently to this material. We hope that the information, exercises, and journaling in *Lifework* will help clients learn from these different responses and facilitate their journey. Any reactions you have to this workbook are welcome. Please send your comments to our attention at:

  University Counseling Center
  Box 564
  University of Notre Dame
  Notre Dame, IN 46556.

Screening Clients for Adult Children Therapy Groups

If a client who happens to be an adult child comes in for assistance with a specific problem, such as writing a resumé, conducting a job search, or negotiating a conflict with a colleague, we feel it is important to respect the client's need to focus on the specific problem and provide the requested assistance, such as information or skill development. It is easy when you first start to offer a therapy group for adult children to be anxious about getting enough members. We understand and share that concern. However, the group will function best when each member can see how his or her goals fit with the overall objective of the group. Clients with interpersonal concerns can see that connection, but clients with specific requests may find it more difficult to see how a group will be beneficial. Supporting these clients by listening to what they need and negotiating to get those needs met often gives them important validation. It may also allow them to examine a deeper level of concern, interpersonal dynamics for example, that may lend itself to a group experience at a later date.

It is also important to screen carefully individuals who specifically request group treatment. Be sure that the motivation to be in a therapy group is not a strategy to avoid dealing with issues that may have been or could be confronted in individual treatment. Some clients want to be in group so they can help others, but have little motivation to focus on themselves.

There are a number of key issues to be considered when determining whether an individual is ready to join a therapy group. Specifically, we appraise the client's feelings of shame, denial of family dynamics, commitment, situational crises, and boundary violations.

Shame: Clients whose shame would prevent them from sharing or keeping the commitment of weekly attendance initially may benefit more from individual work. Individual counseling can give them an opportunity to get comfortable with the therapy process and to learn how to talk about their pain before entering a group.

Family dynamics: Clients who have not acknowledged to themselves that their own family is not functioning well are often overwhelmed by the stories of other group members. Once they can see their family as dysfunctional, they are more able to tolerate group tension and differences without feeling overwhelmed in group.

Commitment: Clients' willingness and ability to commit to attending each group session, even if they have had a bad week, is essential to group cohesion. Clients who cannot or will not make this commitment should not be included in a group.

Situational crises: Some clients have so many situational crises in their lives, such as the need to find another place to live, to figure out how to pay bills, to develop a plan to protect siblings, and so on, that these needs might get lost in a group session in which many members must share group time. Clients with pressing situational needs may benefit more from individual support until they have worked through the crisis period. Referral to group can be delayed until their lives are more stable.

Boundary violations: It is not surprising that clients from dysfunctional families have problems setting appropriate boundaries and limits in their relationships. We have found that the degree of difficulty this issue causes in a client's life needs to be examined. Clients who are so anxious that others' pain feels like their own are not ready for the group experience. If you feel the client will be unable to hear others' painful stories without reacting with extreme stress and anxiety, that client will need help learning how to detach before entering a group. On the other hand, group can be a very appropriate treatment for clients who want to take care of other people at their own expense, who can acknowledge that this is true and recognize their need to learn how to set limits.

We also review the following criteria when determining whether or not a therapy group would be appropriate or less appropriate for an individual adult child. This list was generated during an intern seminar on group therapy at the University Counseling Center at Notre Dame.

(It is important to emphasize here that we are talking now about a therapy group led by professionals and not a Twelve Step group. There are no criteria for joining a Twelve Step group such as ACoA or ACA, except the desire to work on recovery.)

Adult Children Therapy Group Intake Checklist

Appropriate for Therapy Group

- has interpersonal problems
- struggles with comparing self to others
- could benefit from getting feedback from peers
- is too intellectual and could benefit from developing a feeling base
- has high motivation
- is in a reasonable degree of discomfort
- can benefit from helping others
- self-discloses to significant others in his or her life
- is socially isolated
- has made a decision (e.g., to break up a relationship) or needs to accept a reality (e.g., death of a friend) and could benefit from support for the psychological and social transitions involved
- therapist sees attractive qualities in client that will facilitate his or her connection to others, but that may be hidden by pain, coping style, or defensiveness

Less Appropriate

- is actively psychotic
- is schizoid or schizophrenic
- is suspicious and paranoid
- lacks ego strength
- somaticizes (expresses emotions through physical symptoms)
- is excessively needy
- expresses anger in explosive outbursts
- is extremely narcissistic and unable to share group time with others
- is experiencing a major depression
- is suicidal
- is in crisis at intake
- has active substance abuse
- expresses high denial of issues identified at intake (e.g., believes family is perfect and loving)
- lacks any insight into why he or she may be feeling the way he or she does
- is so shy he or she would be unwilling to participate in the group
- has an issue that would benefit from short-term individual intervention (e.g., time management, academic difficulty, test anxiety) that group time would not provide a consistent and specific focus for
- would be considered group deviant because of a language barrier, cultural issues, disability, etc. (This should be assessed with care!)
- expresses maladaptive self-disclosure, either tells everything or nothing about self at inappropriate times
- is fearful of other clients' stories and their pain

The Screening Interview

We are firmly convinced that much of the success of an adult children therapy group depends on what happens before you ever get the group of people together in a room for the first time, which is why screening for appropriate members is so vital to the effectiveness of the group. If, after reviewing the appropriate/less appropriate criteria, you believe she or he may be suited to this kind of group therapy, you still will want to conduct a screening interview with him or her.

We present the interview to the client as an opportunity for therapists and client to determine together whether group is the most helpful way to meet the client's needs at this time. We ask clients to provide background information and explain how they learned about the group and what their expectations, concerns, and fears regarding group participation are. We introduce the idea that our family is the first group we participate in and emphasize that learning and understanding how we coped in our original family will be important information to examine in the group. We discuss how caring and anger were expressed in their family of origin and how those experiences might influence how they react to other group members and the therapists. We ask clients to be willing to bring their most obnoxious self to group and learn to trust that they will be accepted, flaws and all.

An important step in the screening interview is to help clients re-frame their concerns into group goals. For example, if a client mentions that one of her struggles is difficulty trusting others and developing intimate relationships, it is helpful to examine how she reveals her mistrust (e.g., not talking, talking about unimportant issues, joking, focusing on others) and discuss how she would like the therapists and group members to respond when she displays these behaviors. We believe that most coping styles—in this case, being mistrustful—were developed as adaptive survival skills and performed a useful function at one time. It is our task to help clients see how and why these behaviors are no longer helpful and to share our belief that group can be a place to try new behaviors and learn who can and who cannot be trusted.

We also raise the important issue of commitment in the screening interview. For the group to develop into a cohesive, functioning unit, members need to believe they will be able to count on each other, something they often missed in their family of origin. We lay out a specific expectation in terms of a time commitment (for example, ninety-minute sessions once a week for three months) and emphasize that we do not want them in the group unless they can make this commitment a priority in their lives during this time. We predict that there will be times when they won't want to come to group and explain that it will be most important to come on those days to explore why they feel that way. An important lesson a group member can learn when he or she comes to a session and does not want to work is how to ask for space and trust that this request will be respected.

We also explain that the group is different if even one member is missing. Group members learn to count on each other and this makes attendance important. We ask members to let us know if they are unable to make it to a group session so we can announce it to the group. However, the following week it is the member's responsibility to be accountable to the group for why he or she missed the session. We explain during the screening that one of the most hurtful things that can happen to a group is to have a member leave without talking about it and saying good-bye. We ask that if a member feels he or she needs to leave the group, this issue be raised in group so that the group has an opportunity to respond and say good-bye if the member does, in fact, choose to leave.

The better prepared members are during the screening interview and the more aware they are of how their goals can be achieved in group, as well as how each member is responsible for the success of the group, the less likely members are to drop out.

Structuring the Group

Size: We have found that no less than six and no more than ten members is an optimal group size (with two therapists).

Format: We have chosen a closed format. We screen a certain number of members and start everyone in group at the same time for a committed period, usually three months. At the end of that period, we re-evaluate individual goals. Some members choose to continue and others terminate. If new members are added to an ongoing group, we try to add at least two new members at a time.

The beginning of group gives members a chance to tell their stories, and a major focus is grieving over there-and-then feelings about how their lives were affected by someone else's drinking and behaviors. This is a vital step which should not be skipped or minimized. The advantage of continuing this work in a group format is the recognition that current feelings and reactions are tied to the past. We have found that those members who choose to commit to a second three-month period benefit from feeling safe enough in the ongoing group to focus more on here-and-now feelings. Being able to identify those feelings and risk saying them out loud gives clients a way to learn healthy ways of interacting and responding.

Setting Expectations: Our goal in the first session is to provide a safe environment where therapeutic work can take place. We review clients' rights—voluntary participation, respect for individual differences, protection from harm, confidentiality—providing additional individual support when needed and valuing their input when evaluating the group at the end of each time period. We also review clients' responsibilities—to actively participate, to attend all sessions, to let the group know if they plan on dropping out, to speak up if unhappy with the way group is progressing, and to be respectful of others. This information helps clients know what to expect and gives the message that this group experience will not be chaotic, abusive, or disrespectful. This, for many members, is a vast change from their original family environments.

Since members had a chance to think about their goals and re-frame them into appropriate group goals during the screening interview, the way each member introduces himself/herself in the first session provides additional reinforcement and instills hope that each member has appropriate goals that can, in fact, be addressed in a group format. This is not the time for members to say they are not sure why they came or that they have no goals because this will make others less inclined to reveal themselves. If we anticipate that a member will struggle with this in the first group session, we role-play this in the screening interview to prepare him or her.

After members discuss their goals, we point out similarities and differences and encourage them to ask each other questions to get to know each other better. It is important to give members a chance to tell their stories and to accept that there will be differences in how quickly each member will disclose his or her secrets.

Therapy Group Process

We found that using *Lifework* as a way to educate and as a tool for helping clients identify and feel their feelings was especially helpful when assembling a group of individuals who did not understand the dynamics of alcoholism and dysfunctional families and the impact this has had on their lives.

We developed the following sample outline to use *Lifework* in a twelve-week group. We start each session reviewing the previous *Lifework* assignment. Sometimes this generates enough responses to determine the agenda for the session; other times, reactions from previous sessions or to outside life events influences how the group will proceed.

While we do provide an educational function, our primary goal is to help each member take *Lifework* and personalize it to fit his or her life experience. For instance, when reviewing the Path of Recovery section, we have each member circle the statements that are most descriptive of his or her experience. We encourage members to use the journal section to process their reactions to group, to write poetry, do artwork, describe their week, and to chart changes in where they are on the path of recovery so that they can see their own progress. This provides an unstructured way to express themselves and encourages them to be spontaneous and react to themselves instead of others' structures and expectations.

Some clients respond more positively to the open-ended process portion of the group meeting, while others prefer the structure *Lifework* provides. As therapists, we found the greatest advantage of using *Lifework* is that it quickly provides members with a common language to describe their experience, which in turn enhances their ability to support each other. When a member feels stuck, we often suggest that he or she re-read a specific section and see if looking at the concern from that vantage provides additional insight.

Adult Children Therapy Group Outline

WEEK ONE

Getting the help you need and recovery work

Assignment for Week Two

- Review pages 2–20
- Read pages 21–27
- Read pages 47–49

WEEK TWO

Recovery work (continued)

Assignment for Week Three

WEEK THREE

Path of Recovery

Assignment for Week Four

- Draw family home and reactions - pages 56–59
- Family relationships and family losses - pages 60–65

WEEK FOUR

Assignment - Unfinished business, behavioral themes, and change plans - pages 66–74

WEEK FIVE

Assignment - Inventory of strengths and gifts - page 75

WEEK SIX

Assignment - Shame, fear, and anger - pages 79–94

WEEK SEVEN

Assignment - Powerlessness, rage, and depression - pages 95–101

WEEK EIGHT

Assignment - Hope, validation, surrender, and embracing the void - pages 102–110

WEEK NINE

Assignment - Grief, forgiveness, acceptance, and self-love - pages 111–126

WEEK TEN

Assignment - Individuation, appropriate guilt, and healthy anger - pages 127–135

WEEK ELEVEN

Assignment - Aftercare plans and goals - pages 161–165

WEEK TWELVE

Termination

We hope that these guidelines will provide you with some ideas of how you can integrate *Lifework* into your ongoing work with clients who are adult children of alcoholics or otherwise dysfunctional families.

About the Authors

Sally Coleman, who has more than twenty years of counseling experience, is coordinator of addictions services and staff psychotherapist at Notre Dame's University Counseling Center, where she provides individual and group psychotherapy. She is an adult children group facilitator and trainer, a trainer of interns and doctoral students in addictions, a workshop presenter and trainer in areas of grief and loss, and a co-facilitator of therapy groups for religious leaders. A graduate of Marquette University, Milwaukee, with a master's degree in counseling psychology from the University of Notre Dame, she is certified nationally as an addictions counselor. She is former Michigan coordinator of Parkside Lutheran Center for Substance Abuse in Park Ridge, Illinois.

For more than eleven years, Sally Coleman has conducted workshops on adolescent and adult assessment of substance abuse and intervention, victimization, healing through creative visualization, sexual addiction, AIDS, codependency and family recovery, conflict resolution, and grief and loss. She has trained with Elaine Goldman in psychodrama at Camelback Hospital, Scottsdale, Arizona, and with Elizabeth Kübler-Ross in a program for grief facilitators.

Published books by Sally Coleman include *Seasons of the Spirit,* Meditations for Midlife and Beyond, with Maria Porter, and *Our Best Days,* Meditations for Young Adults, with Nancy Hull-Mast (both from Parkside Press), and the original edition of Lifework, published by Ave Marie Press, Notre Dame.

She is a member of the National Association of Alcoholism and Drug Abuse Counselors and Michigan Association of Alcoholism and Drug Abuse Counselors.

Rita J. Donley is an assistant director of the University of Notre Dame Counseling Center, where she also serves as coordinator of clinical services and staff psychologist. A graduate of Ohio State University in social work, she holds an M.A. from the same university in student personnel work and counseling psychology and a Ph.D. in counseling psychology from Pennsylvania State University. She also provides outpatient therapy to private clients at Stress Recovery Center, South Bend, Indiana.

Rita Donley has taught group dynamics to masters and doctoral students in the counseling psychology program at Notre Dame and has participated in team-teaching counseling courses at Ohio State University, Pennsylvania State University, and University of Delaware.

She has been a presenter at several conferences, on such topics as sexual addiction, career development, and professional single women achieving balance. Her professional affiliations include American Psychological Association, Association for Counseling and Development, American College Personnel Association, Association for Specialists in Group Work, and American Group Psychotherapy Association. She is a licensed psychologist in the state of Indiana, and is a health service provider in psychology.

The Twelve Steps of Alcoholics Anonymous

1. We admitted we were powerless over alcohol—that our lives had become unmanageable.

2. Came to believe that a Power greater than ourselves could restore us to sanity.

3. Made a decision to turn our will and our lives over to the care of God, as we understood Him.

4. Made a searching and fearless moral inventory of ourselves.

5. Admitted to God, to ourselves, and to another human being the exact nature of our wrongs.

6. Were entirely ready to have God remove all these defects of character.

7. Humbly asked Him to remove our shortcomings.

8. Made a list of all persons we had harmed, and became willing to make amends to them all.

9. Made direct amends to such people wherever possible, except when to do so would injure them or others.

10. Continued to take personal inventory and when we were wrong, promptly admitted it.

11. Sought through prayer and meditation to improve our conscious contact with God, as we understood Him, praying only for knowledge of His will for us and the power to carry that out.

12. Having had a spiritual awakening as the result of these steps, we tried to carry this message to alcoholics, and to practice these principles in all our affairs.

The Twelve Steps are reprinted with permission of Alcoholics Anonymous World Services, Inc. Permission to reprint does not mean that AA has reviewed or approved the content of this publication, nor that AA agrees with the views expressed herein. AA is a program of recovery from alcoholism—use of the Twelve Steps in connection with programs and activities which are patterned after AA, but which address other problems, does not imply otherwise.